"PERCY"

WINNING IN LIFE

BY

Percy

&

HELEN POWELL WHITE

Helen Powell White

Published
By
Ash Grove Publishing
Diamond, Ohio 44412

Library of Congress
Cataloging-in-Publication Data

Library of Congress Control Number: 2013902169

Copyright © 2013 by Helen Powell White

ISBN-13   978-0-615-77207-3
ISBN-10   0615772072

Printed in the United States By
BOOKMASTERS
30 Amberwood Parkway, Ashland, OH 44805
JOB # M10803 - June 2013

First Edition – 2013

Dedicated to Our Donkey "Sardi"

Many years they traveled
Sardi and his lady fair
Each to the other devoted
Enriching the lifes they shared.

Ashley came to walk one day
She found his charm was real
He eyed this pretty maiden
And tried her heart to steal.

~ + ~

Resident of 'Hotel Sardonia' for years and years,
Sardi enjoyed room service and reminded us daily how
precious love in life can be. The emotional tremolo in his
bray still echoes in the minds and hearts of those he
trusted and loved. Always patient and glad you were
there, Sardi was a beloved pet and a star at 'Ash Grove'.

Forever gentle you humble beast
We loved you well, now rest in peace.

THE TALE

OF

A

TEDDY ROOSEVELT TERRIER

The Enchanted Cottage at Ash Grove

Once again we meet our Teddy Roosevelt Terrier named "Percy". Over the years while keenly engaged in life he has watched the world around him and learned many valuable lessons. He has had the opportunity to be with children. Percy enjoys their enthusiasm and they enjoy him.

With a mind of his own, sweet, eager personality and friendly greeting Percy is sure to become your friend. Who can resist his short little tail vibrating and his chubby little rump wiggling? He can make you smile!

Possessing unusual talents because he lives in The Enchanted Cottage, Percy is going to break his silence and tell us in his own words stories about his life and adventures.

His human mother will add some measured words of wisdom with hopes they will be clearly understood and taken to heart.

In his own words, Percy begins:

"Hi everyone!

I am so glad you are here. My stories should interest you. They are adventures that have shaped my life. When you see my ears ^-^ listen carefully and remember what is said. These are TEDDY TIPS that will greatly help you succeed in life! I want the very best for you!

First, I would like to tell you about myself. I am a Teddy Roosevelt Terrier. In our breed I am known as a "Teddy". I am full of energy, quick, smart, and very loving. Although I do not stand tall, I feel like a big dog. I am strong and well built. You would be surprised to see how far and high I can jump.

Some people have told me I am built like a rock. Rocks don't fly and I think I can (only kidding). Having short legs and being somewhat stocky I am sometimes misjudged.

ᴧ‑ᴧ   TEDDY TIP #1

Never make up your mind about something or someone until you know the facts. If you pre-judge you could be very wrong.

Looking at me you might be fooled.

I understand you are coming for a visit.
I will meet you at the entrance to 'Ash Grove'.
Come on in!

Since it is a freezing cold day I am wearing my red coat to help stay warm. It is always fun to be outside. I love the fresh air and the chance to run.

At Ash Grove where we live, there are lots of interesting places to explore. Let's look around for a little while. It certainly is a beautiful day! Over there, do you see what I see?

Look quickly, as she will be gone in a flash!

In the winter rabbits also run around in the cold and snow. Some of them live in our woods and fields. I dream about chasing them and today their tracks are fresh. Because I have natural hunting instincts, I would love to find a rabbit. My ability comes from a keen sense of smell, excellent sight, agility and speed. I'm sure you also have talents.

ᴧ–ᴧ   TEDDY TIP #2
Use your talents wisely!
Develop these gifts to help you succeed in life.

Right now my paws are feeling numb.
Finding a rabbit will have to wait. We should
head inside to warm up by the fire.

I'll give you a head start and I bet I can
beat you to the door. Ready - Set - Go!

Hurry! I'm waiting!

I want you to meet Mother and Dad.

Larry and Helen

Welcome to 'The Enchanted Cottage'. Whenever we enter this door we feel a spell. LOVE is the spell. Whoever comes will find wonderful feelings of true acceptance, happiness and peace. Here we feel appreciated, cared for, safe and free to be who we are. All of us have trials and troubles, but in The Enchanted Cottage life is special! Our happiness is created by our attitude and how we treat one another. We listen to each other, understand each other and respect each other's feelings.

Please come on inside!

Mother and Dad have plans for the day so they will be leaving us. We will have lots of time to talk and enjoy each other's company. See how nice the fire is! My paws are feeling better already. We can warm up and talk for a while.

Some of you know how long and hard I worked toward earning a United Kennel Club, Companion Dog Title. I finally did it!

It wasn't easy and I didn't quit. It took many lessons, lots of practice and a number of attempts to pass the tests for the title. Here's a picture of me relaxing at the show grounds having just passed the final test. I was thinking about the achievement and enjoying satisfaction in the moment. I had finally accomplished my goal. But I knew I would never stop learning!

ʌ‗ʌ   TEDDY TIP #3

Meet challenges with your very best effort!
Then you can move forward knowing that you have done your best, no matter the outcome.

I would like to tell you about one of my sports. I am learning to run agility courses at Youngstown All Breed Training Club.

This sport uses many obstacles such as a teeter-totter, tunnels, a chute, high walk plank, jumps and weave poles. We follow courses arranged in various patterns marked by numbers on cones. Here's my class. My teacher is on the far right with her two dogs.

Front LtoR: Cheryl & 'Sadie', Kathy &'Molly', Susanne & 'Mae', in pink Barb & 'Roxie', Maria & 'Dreamer', Helen & 'Percy', behind in green-Jill with 'Misty Blue', then Debora with 'Jenna' & 'Jagger', -smiling, Sandy in red with 'Sweet Pea', and our teacher Sharon with gentle 'Shilah' & her patiently waiting, rocket man, 'Rugby'

We like to cheer each other on with team spirit!

My favorite obstacle is the tunnel, because terriers like to go underground to hunt. I get very excited when I see the tunnel. In fact sometimes I get so excited that I get carried away. I yip too much and run around wildly. One day in class, I really got out of hand. It wasn't pleasant. I wrote a letter to my real brothers, Arthur and Lance, to tell them what happened. I knew they would understand.

Ramblewood Kennel TRT's
South Carolina

Dear Brothers Lance and Arthur,

I hope you had a better day today, than I had. Mother and I went to Agility Class this morning. I was up and raring to go. When it was our turn to run the course, I got too excited and started to yip very loud and often. I yipped and yipped and ran around willy-nilly. I was out of control.

My teacher, Miss Sharon, stepped in and told my mother to make me stop. She said, "Do not let Percy boss you around. He is trying to run the show. It is supposed to be a team effort." Oops, my wild behavior was bad!

We started over and when I again couldn't resist the urge to yip and yip louder, all of a sudden, I found myself lying on the floor on my side, with my mother holding me down, staring at me with a stern look on her face. I was very surprised! You might say shocked! I did not think I was being that bad. But after two times being firmly put down on my side, I decided to cool it and quiet down. Big lesson learned! When you are out of control, get a grip. Time out, quiet down, figure out why it happened and try not to have it happen again. My mother and my teacher were pleased to see me learn this lesson. Now I feel better, having told you. It was quite a shocking experience. I thought I was the boss and I learned otherwise.

Love, your brother,

Percy

P.S. I know I will have to work hard to overcome my wild behavior. I don't think it will happen overnight.

˄–˄ TEDDY TIP #4
Mistakes happen. Learn from them.
A life lesson, "To The Stars Through Difficulties"
In Latin: 'ad astra per aspera'

Do things THE RIGHT WAY,
THE FIRST TIME and
ALWAYS ON TIME!

Such advice holds true in agility as in life. To win at this sport you have to complete the course correctly. There are rules and the fastest dog wins. The award does not go to the pokey one or the one who makes errors. I try to do my best yet sometimes that is very hard.

However, because I know obedience commands, I am trusted in some difficult situations. For instance, when we go to get the mail, I am trusted to wait alone inside our gates while mother goes to the box. I often see cars traveling on the road and sometimes I even smell a rabbit nearby. How tempting to think of leaving and going to check. But I do not move a muscle. This takes great self-control.

∧‒∧　TEDDY TIP #6

Be dependable in every way.
Do what you say and always follow through!

Now I'd like to tell you how important it is to have a friend. I had Winston. We were real buddies! I could tell him anything and his 'Winnie kisses' were the best! I was very sad when he died. He was so kind to me and we meant so much to each other.

∧‗∧   TEDDY TIP #7

When loss breaks your heart, try to find your smile and think of happy precious memories.

Look for new beginnings! *I needed to get over my sadness. Mother and Dad decided we should adopt another Teddy Roosevelt Terrier.*

I remember the day they went to choose a puppy. One brave little fellow ran over to my mother, crawled up on her lap and kissed her. Without words he said, "I want you to pick me!" She did and brought home my new brother, Weebits Whisper "Sweet Simon".

When I first met Simon I sniffed his nose and told him everything would be all right. I saw his little tail wiggle in reply. We have become best friends.

ᴧ–ᴧ TEDDY TIP #8
Choose a friend wisely.
A friend should bring out the best in you.

A friend shares the good and the bad in life. Good friends help to make each other's lives better. Family you inherit, friends you earn.

Simon and I play together and we also guard our home. No mouse, chipmunk, rabbit, squirrel or cat is going to come close without us letting everyone know. We are a team and we think we could scare off a burglar if needed.

However the evening can be a scary time for me. When I think about certain things my heart races and my thoughts run wild. I have very good hearing and at night I hear sounds that frighten me. My mother will tell you:

"Thumps and bumps, rumbles and growls
Lights in the dark and faraway howls
Alert little Percy to bark and to stare
Wondering, wondering, who is out there?"

A friend, who was a policeman, gave me some
very good advice on how to keep safe. He said,
"Do not go where you are not supposed to be."

In the evening we are not allowed to run outside in the big unfenced yard that is surrounded by woods. We can only go in the small courtyard where there is a high fence, gates and a bright light. Mother told me, danger lurks in the dark beyond this space.

Raccoons, that can be very vicious, travel through the yard at night. Sometimes skunks are there with spray that has a terrible odor. And fox live in the woods nearby and they hunt for prey at night.

Dad said my barking at night might call in a hungry coyote. The coyote could wait in the dark for me to make a mistake by going out of the courtyard. I don't like to think about that!

It is very clear that we do not belong out in the big yard or out in the woods in the dark.

There are other places where we should not go alone, like out by the road at anytime. I am smart and understand the reasoning. I want to keep safe and out of trouble.

OK creatures of the night, this is what we would do to you!

ᴧ–ᴧ   TEDDY TIP #9
HEED WARNINGS!
Think Before You Act.

To get my mind off scary thoughts I have a place I want to show you. We have been sitting here for a while. Seeing it for yourself is better than telling you about it.

Let's head out.

As you look down the driveway you will see a building we call 'The Wigwam'. A wigwam is an American Indian hut or lodge. In this building there is a room with interesting tools, pottery, beadwork, baskets and weavings made by Indians. They give us a glimpse into their culture. Indians have an important place in our country and we will find an Indian in there waiting to greet us. He is a very big chief. He looks right at you but he never says a word. Here, take a look! He is very stern and gruff but I can tell you he is not alive. With my good sense of smell, I have checked him out.

Mother likes to recall the old Indian parable of 'The Two Wolves'. It is a lesson a wise old Cherokee grandfather gave to his grandson.

"My Son there is A BATTLE between
Two wolves, inside us all.

One is EVIL.
It is anger, jealousy, greed,
resentment, inferiority, lies and ego.

The other is GOOD.
It is joy, peace, love, hope, humility,
kindness, empathy and truth."

The boy thought about it and asked.
"Grandfather which wolf wins?"
The old man quietly replied,

"The one you feed."

ʌ–ʌ   TEDDY TIP #10:

DEVELOP ALL QUALITIES OF GOOD.
Your character will thrive.
Your life will shine with goodness.

RECOGNIZE EVIL IN ALL ITS WAYS!
And keep it out of your life.

*****MAKE GOOD CHOICES*****

Now let's go back to the house. You have seen the Indian Chief and heard his message. The moral of his story is very important!

I would like to tell you about some other outstanding people I have met and I have pictures to show you.

We'd better be a little careful as we walk back down the driveway as the fresh snow has made it slippery. Here we are. And here are the pictures I want you to see.

My first photo is of a group of men who possess fine values. These men have chosen 'Good over Evil.' They are disciplined, well trained and very respected. They are retired Veterans of our Armed Forces. It was a privilege to meet them at the dedication of their new kiosk. We gathered around for this picture to record my visit. I will never forget them.

Retired Military War Veterans, St. Peter of the Fields, Rootstown, Ohio

These soldiers understand the dangers of war and possess patriotism, courage and valor. What good choices they have made in their lives! Men and women in our Armed Forces love our country, uphold our laws, respect our flag, honor and defend our country and our freedoms. They are loyal comrades. We honor them and we can never thank them enough.

I have been fortunate to meet some younger men who are currently on the road to success. They are in the Boy Scouts of America. I have one friend in particular who inspires me. He just earned his Eagle Scout and will be admired for life for this accomplishment.

Eagle Scout Michael Allman and Percy

I also got to meet a troop of Scouts in our neighborhood. My mother and I visited them one evening and shared our stories.

They are fine young men, learning to be responsible, self-reliant and prepared for life. Scouts earn merit badges in a large variety of subjects, interests and skills. They camp, explore, study, travel and learn to do many things. Scouting shapes lives for success in life!

B.S.A. Troop 105, North Jackson, Ohio under the leadership of Scoutmaster Alex Kegley

I gladly returned their warm welcome! When in trouble I want a Scout around. A Scout will know what to do and how to help.

We particularly like the 4-H organization because family members were in it for years. I am not allowed to go to their Fair as I am not a member but we have some pictures. 4-H stands for Head, Heart, Hands, and Health. Young people can join a variety of clubs. Clubs for livestock, hobbies and many more subjects, offer knowledge, skills and fun.

18 USC 707

WE'RE HELPING FUTURE LEADERS TO GROW!

4-H Jonathon and "Moonshine"   The Famous 'Randolph Fair' Ohio   4-H Jessica with her horse "Baby"

In the summer beside 4-H Fair, picking blueberries is a favorite pass time for my mother and her friend JoAnn. They often meet early in the morning at Wolff's Farm when it is cool and the berries are ripe and plump. There they met Amber Wolff who is a Girl Scout leader. The three arranged a get-together for us to meet the Girl Scouts. Simon was to come along. When the time came he was very excited! I told him to be on his best behavior and he was. Timmy took pictures while I got to sit on JoAnn's lap.

Thanks Timmy! Happiness comes in pairs!

Visiting Troop 91010 was a very happy
time! The girls are busy with many projects.
Plans for selling those delicious GS cookies,
summer camp, community service projects, such
as a yard sale and food drive for the needy, are
underway. What a great group of girls!

Girl Scouts provides a place for young
girls/young ladies to develop their skills, share
goals with fellow scouts and achieve fine levels
of responsibility and personal leadership.

May their dreams come true!

My next adventure was with a group of special teenagers, the Senior Youth Group at our church. In Faith based groups nationwide young people share common beliefs and values.

I joined them on a retreat, and immediately sensed the close friendships. This togetherness is important! Life is easier and more fun when you support one another! These kids assist at church, aid charities, do food drives and visit nursing homes. They are super teenagers!

Here I am with the thirteen teenagers who belong to the group. By the smiles you know we all had fun!

Our Leader

I got to meet everyone and see everything that was going on.

It was nice to end my visit on a high note.   *I think I made a friend!*

ᴧ‒ᴧ   TEDDY TIP #11

JOIN A GROUP OR A TEAM THAT HAS HIGH GOALS AND WHOLESOME ACTIVITY. IF YOU SERIOUSLY TAKE PART YOU CAN BENEFIT!
ALWAYS
REMEMBER TO HOLD TRUE TO YOUR MORALS AND VALUES AND NEVER ALLOW YOURSELF TO GET DRUG ALONG IN A PACK! (Beware of Bad Wolves.)

I also know how very important it is to be kind and caring. I often crawl onto laps and give gentle kisses. Being tender is easy for me because I am happiest giving love and being loved in return.

Some of you may remember our Rottweiler "Ginger". She visited nursing homes for many years. Wearing her bandana she was known as 'Miss Kissy" as she cheered the elderly. There are many other ways to show kindness.

Recently we learned about a crippled dog named "Gramercy". When I saw his picture I saw terrier resemblance to me and thought, oh dear! What if I needed help! He needs help! Without hesitation we joined his case. Gramercy has a foster family of very kind people associated with New Rattitude Rat Terrier Rescue. He seriously needs surgery for

a chance to live free of pain. Now strangers
who are compassionate and love dogs are
joining in to help. I have his picture.

Gramercy

By helping to pay for his doctors and his surgery he has a chance for a comfortable life. He will never be able to do terrier races as I do.

PERCY at Premier 2012 trying out the course.

But he will know people care.

Everywhere in the world there is need for charity. Look around and follow your heart. Somewhere, someone is waiting in need!

ᴧ–ᴧ   TEDDY TIP # 12

CARE AND COMFORT
GIVE FREELY
A GENEROUS SPIRIT SOARS!

Before you leave I have one last story to tell you. It still amazes me for I never imagined it would happen, never in my wildest dreams!

Thus far in life, my tractor, 'High Steppin Sam', has given me thrills. Riding on top of that big machine is awesome! I have often wondered what it would be like to ride on a giant fire truck. Just the thought of being up on such a truck gets me excited! If I got to meet a fireman and go for a ride on a fire truck that would be the thrill of a lifetime!

Let me tell you, it happened because I reached for that dream by writing a letter to our Fire Chief. He read my letter and presented it to the Township Trustees and the members voted and approved my request. I was invited to ride on a Big Beautiful Fire Truck!

Here is a shortened copy of my letter that won the day!

April 13, 2012

Palmyra Township Fire Department

Dear Chief,

This may be the most unusual letter you ever receive, because it comes from a dog. My name is Percy.

Dreams and ambitions are important in life. My mother asked me what my dream in life would be? I told her I wanted to ride on a Fire Truck. I know how brave you firemen are. I know stories of rescues and how you help people. You are brave and courageous! I would love to meet you. It would be an honor.

I dream one day of getting to ride on a fire truck. You can ask people who know me and they will tell you I love to ride on our big tractor.

If you could make my dream come true, I would like to tell about it in my final book. As firemen, you set such a fine examples of winning in life.

Thank you for considering my request. Please take all the time you need to discuss this with your men. I will look forward to your reply.

Most Sincerely,

Percy

It was just before The Fourth of July when we met the Chief and a Lieutenant Fireman at the Fire Station. Flags were flying, the sun was shining, and I was the happiest dog in town! We were helped up into the truck because it was so high. What a thrill!

As we rumbled out of the station and down the road I could feel the power beneath us!

The Chief used his radio to report our position.

We then stopped at the Township Park to take pictures so I could always remember this day.

The Chief and Lieutenant became my heroes. For the memory of a lifetime, I bark thanks to them and all the people who made the ride possible! Our community is special!

Chief Mark Garvin

Lieutenant Derek Reed

Firemen are very brave. They put their lives on the line to protect property and rescue people and animals from harm. They deserve great respect, as do all brave individuals who at times face danger. And respect is due people who use their intelligence, skills and talents in other ways to help us. Who would you name?

Look, my dream came true!

ʌ_ʌ   TEDDY TIP # 13

DARE TO DREAM and DREAM BIG, Really **BIG!**

STEP UP & TRY = AMAZING THINGS CAN HAPPEN!

You are leaving now. I hope you learned from my experiences. It takes thought and effort to succeed in life. Years pass so quickly and I trust you will make the best of them. I have a hunch you will! Good-by, good luck!

I SEND MY LOVE! ”

Love can ease pain!   Love can bring joy!   Love can last forever!”

THE END

TEDDY ROOSEVELT TERRIERS on PARADE

To give readers a chance to get better acquainted with the Teddy Roosevelt Terrier, we gathered from around the country some of these beloved dogs that represent the breed and charm the lives of their owners.

Watching from the viewing stand are the Weebits Teddies that started this tale. With two arriving from 'Ramblewood Kennel TRTs', S.C. it is special to see the three brothers together. Theirs is a lifelong bond.

King Arthur   Sir Lancelot   Sir Perceval

Observing the parade with them are Teresa and Tom Otto, the boys' 'human parents'. Many puppies have entered this world into Teresa's loving hands. She and husband Tom give them their best.

Teresa, "Simon" & Tom, then with Sara at UKC Show –Sept. 11, 2011/ Teresa & Helen

Leading the parade today is our Honorary Parade Marshall, Parson's Terrier "Triscuit". She has many fans and has been a long time friend of the TRTerriers. You will remember her from book II.

Stepping out spritely, Triscuit knowlingly eyes the crowd as cheers and clapping are heard. She is followed by the Ohio 'Weebits Teddy Roosevelt Terriers', the loved 'furkids' of Teresa and Tom Otto at ImageEvents.com/weebitsratterriers. Percy's family brother "Sweet Simon" is in the middle, flanked by Simon's parents, "Belle" & "Moose".

CH Weebits Southern Belle   CH Weebits Whisper " Sweet Simon"   CH Weebits Coin of the Relm

From the Great Lakes State of Michigan, march four of Mary Ann May's outstanding 'Brooks N Mays Teddy Roosevelt Terriers'.

These very handsome champions, "Tanka" "Harold" and "Coby", are accompanied today by "Dunbar" who holds a Grand Champion title!

Leading the group is Grand Champion Dunbar, the United Kennel Club's #1 Teddy Roosevelt Terrier in the year 2011. Here is Dunbar. He is special inside and out, being extremely gentle and truly beautiful!

UKC #1 TRT 2011 GRCH Brooks N Mays Dunbar

CH Brooks N Mays Tanka   CH Brooks N Mays   CH Brooks N Mays
                 The Herald Angel   Cobalt Blue

Next appear Teddies to tug at your heart with their expressive eyes. From New York State, 'Prestige Kennels', comes the soulful CH Stars and Stripes Forever, "Tully". And from the Great State of Texas, come two 'TEXAS TRUE BLUES', who are obviously very pleased to be here.

CH Stars and Stripes Forever "Tully"

CH Texas Tumble Weed, "Mindy"

Lazy Daisy Mae

Gracious goodness look who's coming now! Also from The Lone Star State, D. Moore sends his pack of Teddies. His venerable friend "Dooder", properly known as DKM's Mister Dood is front and center. This twelve-year-old TRT comes from an old line of terriers found primarily in Texas. This Texas line is known for it's strong prey drive and hunting instincts. On either side of Mister Dood are his sons.

DKM's Sing R Proud, son of

DKM's Mister Dood

and son, DKM's Snap O'Dooder

Their mother (dam) "Kit" is also here with her "Bobbin" and "Chenille".

The dam Cmon Kit

DKM's Bobbin Blu

DKM's Chenille Sew Fine

'Aspen Hill Farms' in Holly Springs, Mississippi sends three fine Teddies, "Sparky", "Roxie" and "Ellie Mae". Before leaving they had to tell the young ones, they would be playing at home. The pups said, "We want to go!" When the pups grow up they can march and they will. This time only the adults get to go. They will bring home stories.

"But we want to go to!" Aspen's Ellie Mae Aspen's Rockin Robin CH Aspen's Sparticus of CCK

Sparky is already on his feet. "You know there is never a dull moment with us around. We can liven up any scene and particularly a good parade. What fun! Let's go!" This merry band from 'The Deep South' is with us here today.

Doing what they love to do, these Louisiana Teddies from 'Caney Creek Kennel' keep their noses to the ground. Mike Staples sends his handsome, ever admired and loved "Stoney" to appear in The Parade.

Caney Creek Copper   Copper with his son Stoney   GRCH Stonewall Jackson

Jackie Craver of 'Cedar Rose Teddies' in Kentucky sends the spirit of her beloved Grand Champion CDRose Party Time Man, known by many as PTM. He was one very special TRT and his lineage carries on.

PTM as a young dog   GRCH CDRose Party Time Man   GRCH PTM as an adult

In turn, here come more crowd pleasing Teddies. These are from the State of Georgia. They romp and play at 'Barnett's Rambling Terriers' under the wonderful care of Lesa Barnett and her lovely family.
"Zorro" looks left then right yet keeps an ever constant eye on 'his Lesa'.

GRCH Weebits Zorro   Lesa and CH Barnett's Reba Shay   Again GRCH Zorro

Embraced with respect, all the Teddy members of the family hope to follow in Ginger's stellar paw prints. Each one is special!

CH Barnett's RockABye   CH Barnett's   Beloved Ginger   Barnett's "Zeke"
Baylee of CCK   Majestic Macie   Gamblin Man Strikes Again

From coast to coast they come.

Far away in New England, news has spread about The Parade. Hearing that Teddies are marching "Fiona" wants to go.
In a flash she is on the move and makes it here in plenty of time!

Loved by Electra Blair/3bear Farm VT, we introduce Fiona, titled Grand Champion Weebits ahRoot Toot N Good Time! "Go Fifi!"

Arriving from the west coast, from the state of Washington, are the 'Dynamo Teddy Roosevelt Terriers'. These Teddies are family to 'The Little Lady' and her husband, who love and watch over Percy and Simon. It is daughter Sara, her husband Jimmy and the twins who also have Teddy Roosevelt Terriers as family members. With arms full of love we welcome the twin grandchildren, William and Audrey with three outstanding Teddies. Smiling faces and winsome 'furkids' make the day!

William holds Spirit and Snowy, Audrey holds Copper

CH Brooks Snow on Fluorite Ridge

(Pictured separately on the side is Granddaughter Audrey with CH Brooks Snow on Fluorite Ridge, "Snowy". Audrey ranked in the United Kennel Club's Top Ten Junior Showmanship in 2012 with Snowy.)

Marching smartly next, is Sara with UWP CH Dynamo Spirit of Weebits, their special "Spirit". Beyond a title in Conformation, Spirit has also earned a title in Weight Pulling, by pulling over 200 lbs. For a twelve-pound dog this is totally amazing!

"Spirit"

UWP CH Dynamo Spirit of Weebits

The founding member of their Dynamo Team is "Copper". He was the United Kennel Club #1 Teddy Roosevelt Terrier in 2012. His credentials are awesome. With his United Flat Race Champion, United Steeplechase Racer and conformation Grand Champion titles in hand, he is officially know as URCH USR GRCH Weebits Copper Dynamo.

UKC #1 TRT 2012 URCH USR GRCH Weebits Copper Dynamo

Dynamo Teddies keep this family on the go. And they are having a great time at the parade today!

Now we introduce our last parade entry.

Thanks to Teresa, a certain little Teddy Roosevelt Terrier lives on a couch in Pennsylvania with a couple, his family. He has not earned titles or traveled around the country acquiring skills and records. He has simply lived at home, keeping faithful watch and providing enormous love and companionship for his folks and their numerous grandchildren and great grandchildren. He is their dog for life! Raved about by his family, he is proof that a dog can be a true ray of sunshine in one's life! We know that! Please give a hearty round of applause and cheer for "Teddy" of Weebits is here!

Our parade now ends with a joyful reunion for all!

Wanting to help animals, Percy has donated his books to support the new Animal Welfare Care and Education Center in Trumbull County Ohio. And his books are given to Youngstown All Breed Training Club in North Jackson, Ohio to contribute toward the building of their new, much needed, training facility. Both facilities will greatly better the lives of dogs and others. Contributions to support these and other projects are important and very appreciated! Percy is delighted to do his part!

As Percy shares his stories he enjoys visiting young people in school. Imagine what it is like to be a Teddy Rock Star for classes of third graders? The kids think he is the greatest!

Third Grade Class at Southeast Elementary School, Portage Co. Ohio

Percy has never outgrown his love of the chase. He and Sweet Simon give us a final perspective on their happy lives.

FOLLOW YOUR PATH   HPW
I took my dogs on a woodland stroll
    With nary a care or a stick
Their bouncing heads in gleeful range
    Told me I must be quick
Darting this way, darting back
    They covered the ground through the brush
Simon and Percy had found the trail
    With advancing determined rush
My smile now spread as the rabbit's tail
    Turned and headed west
The boys will have to run real hard
    To catch up with the best
For a rabbit can dart and zig and zag
    And befuddle the frantic chase
But I know these dogs and I know full well
    They're determined to win this race
For ever so clever as terriers are
    They have heart and strength from within
They will not quit or head back home
    Or be content to live in a pen
Their pursuit will proceed, be there bunny or not
    As they take on life as it comes
With Attitude, Effort and Knowledge they know
    "Winning in Life" can be fun!

With values that are universal, Percy hopes
readers, young and old, will find a way . . .

To give inspiration for paths yet to find
To give encouragement for abilities to shine
*****
To give audience for confidence to build
To give love to insure the heart is fulfilled
*****
To take opportunity to walk through life's doors
To take time to learn, to dream and explore
*****
To take care and courage along for the ride
To take knowledge and goodness to be by your side

HER JOURNEY STARTED LONG, LONG AGO, HELEN AND UNCLE ROBERT.

ACKNOWLEDGEMENTS

As a trilogy "PERCY" The Perfect Puppy, "PERCY" Growing Up, and "Percy" Winning In Life are now known as 'The Percy Books'. Thanks to the fine people at BookMasters, Ashland, OH for printing

Jamie Brawlee - photo at SE Elem. School, Palmyra Township, OH

Ruth and Larry Coz - photo of Helen and Larry

Diana, John & Ashley James-Ashley with Sardi, Jonathon/Moonshine

Timmy Henry-inside cover photo of Helen & Percy, plus Girl Scouts

Julee Stearnsallen-"Gramercy"/New Rattitude Rat Terrier Rescue, WA

Cathy & Robin Schwind - Cathy's photo of Helen and Sardi

April Walsh Woolner - photo of Teresa, Mary Ann and Dean in Book 1

Teddy Roosevelt Terrier friends nationwide - photos of your TRTs

Retired Veterans & Sr. Youth Group/ St. Peter of Fields, Rootstown, OH

The Palmyra Township Volunteer Fire Dept. & Trustees, Diamond, OH

BSA Troop 105 with Scoutmaster Alex "Mr. Fish" Kegley,
   Assistant Scoutmasters Chris Fortunato & John Lennox & Scouts:
   James A., Zach B., Robbie C., Kent G., Dylan J., Duncan K.,
   Tibius K., Joshua M., Cameron P., Andrew S., Scott U., & Josh W.

Girl Scout Troop 91010 with Scout Leader Amber Wolff & Scouts:
   McKenna A., Dez M. Kaysha H., Chasidy S., Savannah W.,
   Hannah W., Kourtney B., Hallie S. & Sarah W.

4-H Portage County OH, '10th Cavalry' member Jessica S.

Youngstown All Breed Training Club, North Jackson, OH- club support
   Joe Stiffler - photo of Percy's Agility class at YABTC

Family/Friends: Sara, Jimmy, Audrey & William Flour,
Charles Victor Lang & Sandy, Lesa Barnett, Sue Brumbaugh, JoAnn F.,
Maria & Chris Gesing, Timmy Henry, CeCe & Ray Knispel, Bruce
Knodel, Nancy & Frank Liszka, Mary Ann May, Reverend David
Misbrener, Teresa & Tom Otto, Sharon Phillips, Bernadette Przybylski,
Sherry Shay, Dolores & Robert Winkler & dear friends at YABTC.

Your valued and enthusiastic support has been deeply appreciated!
We thank you all and with Larry's Polish heritage we wish you well!
"Idz a Bogien" = "Go with God"